# Impact investing strategies

# Aligning Financial Goals with Social and Environmental Goals

Matthew E. Dalton

All rights reserved. No part of this publication may be reproduced, distributed, or transmitted in any form or by any means, including photocopying, recording, or other electronic or mechanical methods, without the prior written permission of the publisher, except in the case of brief quotations embodied in critical reviews and certain other noncommercial uses permitted by copyright law.

Copyright © (Matthew E. Dalton), (2023)

# Table of Contents

## CHAPTER ONE

## CHAPTER TWO

## CHAPTER THREE

## CHAPTER FOUR

## CHAPTER FIVE

## CHAPTER SIX

# CHAPTER ONE

### Impact Investing

Impact investing is a type of investing that seeks to generate both financial returns and positive social or environmental impact. In other words, impact investors aim to achieve a "double bottom line," or a combination of financial success and measurable progress toward addressing social or environmental challenges.

Unlike traditional investing, which focuses solely on financial returns, impact investing considers the broader societal and environmental implications of investments. Impact investors actively seek out opportunities to invest in companies, organizations, and funds that are making a positive impact on the world, while still delivering competitive financial returns.

Impact investing can take many forms, such as investing in renewable energy, sustainable agriculture, or affordable housing. It can also involve investing in companies that prioritize diversity, equity, and inclusion, or those that are working to address healthcare disparities or climate change.

One of the key principles of impact investing is the measurement and reporting of social and environmental impact. Impact investors often use a variety of metrics to assess and communicate the impact of their investments, such as the United Nations Sustainable Development Goals (SDGs), the Global Impact Investing Network's (GIIN) Impact Reporting and Investment Standards (IRIS), or other specialized frameworks.

Overall, impact investing is a growing movement that seeks to align financial interests with social and environmental responsibility, creating positive change in the world while generating financial returns for investors.

Impact investing is a form of investing that seeks to generate both financial returns and positive social or environmental impact. This approach is gaining popularity as investors increasingly look for ways to use their capital to make a positive difference in the world, while still earning a competitive return on their investment.

One of the key features of impact investing is the focus on measurable outcomes. Impact investors typically look for investments that are designed to achieve specific social or environmental goals, and they often use a range of metrics and indicators to track progress toward these goals. These might include indicators such as carbon emissions reduction, access to clean water, or improved healthcare outcomes, among others.

Another important aspect of impact investing is the recognition that social and environmental goals are often interconnected with financial performance. In other words, investments that contribute to positive social or environmental outcomes can also deliver strong financial returns. This alignment of interests can create a virtuous cycle, in which investments that generate both financial and social or environmental benefits are seen as particularly attractive by investors.

Impact investing can take many different forms, from direct investments in social enterprises or non-profits to investments in publicly traded companies that are focused on sustainability and social responsibility. In recent years, several specialized impact investment funds and platforms have emerged, designed to connect impact investors with a range of investment opportunities across different sectors and regions.

Overall, impact investing is a rapidly growing field that reflects a broader shift towards more socially and environmentally responsible investing. As investors become more aware of the impact their capital can have on the world, they are increasingly looking for ways to use their investments to create positive change, while still generating financial returns.

## Growth of Impact Investing

The growth of impact investing reflects a broader shift towards more socially and environmentally responsible investing, as investors recognize the potential of their capital to make a positive difference in the world. As this trend continues to gather momentum, impact investing is likely to play an increasingly important role in shaping the future of finance and business. The growth of impact investing has been driven by a range of factors, including changing attitudes toward the role of business in society, growing awareness of global social and environmental challenges, and the emergence of new technologies and investment structures.

One key driver of the growth of impact investing has been the recognition that traditional models of business and investing may not be well suited to address the complex social and environmental challenges facing the world today. In many cases, these challenges require a more collaborative and multidisciplinary approach, bringing together stakeholders from across the public, private, and non-profit sectors to create innovative solutions. Impact investing is seen as one way to support this kind of collaboration, by providing a way for investors to engage with organizations and projects that are working towards positive social or environmental outcomes.

Another factor driving the growth of impact investing is the increasing recognition of the importance of social and environmental factors in business decision-making. In recent years, a growing number of companies have recognized that investing in sustainability and social responsibility can be good for business, by helping to build customer loyalty, improve employee engagement, and reduce risk. This has led to a proliferation of companies and funds that are focused on sustainability and social responsibility, creating new opportunities for impact investors to engage with these organizations.

The growth of impact investing has also been supported by the emergence of new technologies and investment structures. In recent years, advances in fintech and blockchain have made it easier to invest in impact-focused projects and organizations, by reducing transaction costs and improving transparency. At the same time, new investment structures, such as social impact bonds and development impact bonds, have created new ways to finance social and environmental initiatives, by linking funding to specific outcomes and performance targets.

## Why Impact Investing Matters

Impact investing matters because it provides a way to use finance as a tool for positive change, promoting greater social and environmental responsibility while still delivering strong financial returns. As investors become more aware of the potential of impact investing to create meaningful change, it is likely to play an increasingly important role in shaping the future of finance and business. Impact investing, therefore, matters for several reasons, which can be broadly categorized into three areas: social, environmental, and economic.

From a social perspective, impact investing can help to address some of the most pressing social challenges facing the world today, such as poverty, inequality, and social exclusion. By providing critical funding for organizations and initiatives that are working to create solutions to these complex problems, impact investors can help to promote greater social inclusion, equity, and empowerment.

Moreover, impact investing can also create positive social spillover effects, by driving demand for sustainable products and services, promoting responsible business practices, and catalyzing innovation in areas such as healthcare, education, and affordable housing. These positive spillover effects can benefit both individuals and communities and help to create more sustainable and equitable societies over the long term.

From an environmental perspective, impact investing can help to address some of the most pressing environmental challenges facing the world today, such as climate change, deforestation, and water scarcity. By investing in organizations and initiatives that are working to create solutions to these complex problems, impact investors can help to promote greater environmental sustainability, conservation, and resilience.

Impact investing can help to promote greater transparency and accountability in the financial sector. By focusing on measurable social and environmental outcomes, impact investing can help to create a more rigorous approach to investment evaluation and reporting. This can lead to greater accountability for both investors and organizations and can help to promote more responsible and sustainable investing practices more broadly.

Moreover, impact investing can also create positive environmental spillover effects, by driving demand for sustainable products and services, promoting sustainable business practices, and catalyzing innovation in areas such as clean energy, circular economy, and sustainable agriculture. These positive spillover effects can benefit both individuals and communities and help to create more sustainable and resilient ecosystems over the long term.

From an economic perspective, impact investing can help to create more sustainable and inclusive economies, by promoting greater access to capital, stimulating job creation, and driving innovation in areas such as social enterprise and impact investing. By investing in organizations and initiatives that prioritize social and environmental goals, impact investors can help to create more resilient and adaptive economies, which can better withstand shocks and crises, and promote greater prosperity and well-being for all.

## Understanding the Principles of Impact Investing

Impact investing is an investment approach that aims to generate both financial returns and measurable social and environmental impact. Impact investing is guided by a set of principles that help investors align their financial goals with their social and environmental values. To achieve this dual objective, impact investing is guided by a set of principles that help investors align their financial goals with their social and environmental values. These principles can be broadly categorized into four main areas: intentionality, additionality, measurement, and transparency.

- *Intentionality*

Impact investing is intentional in its pursuit of social and environmental goals. This means that impact investors are actively seeking out investments that align with their values and are committed to making a positive difference in the world. They are focused on creating measurable impact alongside financial returns and are transparent about their social and environmental goals and objectives. By being intentional, impact investors can prioritize investments that generate positive outcomes for society and the environment, rather than simply maximizing financial returns.

- *Additionality*

Impact investing seeks to create additionality, or positive impact that would not have occurred without the investment. This means that impact investors are looking for opportunities to create new solutions to social and environmental challenges, rather than simply financing existing solutions. They are focused on investing in organizations and projects that are innovative, scalable, and have the potential to create lasting change. By creating additionality, impact investors can address social and environmental challenges that have not been adequately addressed by other forms of finance.

- ***Measurement***

Impact investing is committed to measuring and tracking social and environmental impact alongside financial performance. This means that impact investors are using metrics and data to evaluate the effectiveness of their investments in creating positive change. They are focused on understanding the social and environmental outcomes of their investments and using this information to inform future investment decisions. By measuring impact, impact investors can assess the effectiveness of their investments and make informed decisions about future investments.

- ***Transparency***

Impact investing is transparent in its reporting and communication of social and environmental impact. This means that impact investors are committed to reporting on the social and environmental outcomes of their investments and are open about their investment strategies, goals, and objectives. They are focused on building trust and credibility with stakeholders and on promoting greater accountability and responsibility in the financial sector. By being transparent, impact investors can demonstrate the positive impact of their investments and encourage greater participation in the impact investing sector.

## The Importance of Aligning Financial Goals with Social and Environmental Goals

Aligning financial goals with social and environmental goals is important because it can help investors create a positive impact on the world, mitigate risks associated with sustainability issues, access opportunities for long-term value creation, and attract a wider range of investors who are looking for investments that align with their values. It allows investors to create a positive impact on society and the environment while also achieving financial returns. By investing in companies or projects that prioritize social and environmental outcomes alongside financial returns, investors can use their capital to support positive change in the world. There are several reasons why aligning financial goals with social and environmental goals is important:

- ***Positive impact***

Investing in socially and environmentally responsible companies or projects can help to generate positive social and environmental outcomes. For example, investing in a company that produces renewable energy can help reduce carbon emissions and combat climate change. Investing in a company that provides access to clean water can improve public health and well-being. Impact investing provides an opportunity for investors to use their capital to make a positive impact on the world.

- ***Risk management***

Companies that prioritize social and environmental goals may be better positioned to manage risks related to sustainability issues. For example, a company that has strong environmental practices is less likely to face regulatory fines or reputational damage from environmental incidents. By investing in companies with strong social and environmental practices, investors can mitigate risks associated with sustainability issues and improve their portfolio's overall risk profile.

- ***Long-term value creation***

Companies that prioritize social and environmental goals may be better positioned for long-term value creation. For example, companies that focus on environmental sustainability may be better positioned to adapt to a changing regulatory environment or shifting consumer preferences. By investing in companies that prioritize social and environmental goals, investors can access opportunities for long-term value creation.

- *Investor demand*

There is a growing demand among investors for investments that align with their social and environmental values. By aligning financial goals with social and environmental goals, investors can attract a wider range of investors who are looking for investment opportunities that have a positive impact on society and the environment.

## The Growth and Potential Impact of Investing

Impact investing has the potential to make a significant positive impact on society and the environment by supporting companies and projects that prioritize social and environmental outcomes. As the impact investing market continues to grow, impact investors will likely play an increasingly important role in addressing some of the world's most pressing social and environmental challenges.

Impact investing has seen rapid growth in recent years and has the potential to make a significant impact on society and the environment. According to the Global Impact Investing Network (GIIN), the estimated size of the impact investing market is now over $700 billion, with an annual growth rate of approximately 20% over the past five years. This growth is driven by increasing demand from investors who are looking to align their investments with their social and environmental values.

One of the key factors driving the growth of impact investing is the increasing awareness of the need to address pressing social and environmental challenges. Investors are becoming more aware of the role they can play in addressing these challenges through their investment decisions. Impact investing provides a way for investors to make a positive impact on society and the environment while still generating financial returns.

Another factor driving the growth of impact investing is the increasing availability of impact investment opportunities. Impact investing used to be limited to a few specialized funds, but today, there is a wide range of impact investment opportunities available across various asset classes, including private equity, venture capital, and fixed income.

The potential impact of impact investing is vast. By investing in companies and projects that prioritize social and environmental outcomes, impact investors can help to address a wide range of social and environmental challenges. Some of the areas that impact investing can have a significant impact on include:

- ***Climate change***

Impact investing can help to address climate change by supporting companies that are developing renewable energy, improving energy efficiency, and reducing greenhouse gas emissions. By investing in these types of companies, impact investors can help to accelerate the transition to a low-carbon economy.

- ***Sustainable agriculture***

Impact investing can support sustainable agriculture by investing in companies that promote regenerative agriculture, reduce food waste, and increase access to healthy food. By investing in sustainable agriculture, impact investors can help to improve food security and promote sustainable land use.

- ***Financial inclusion***

Impact investing can support financial inclusion by investing in companies that provide access to financial services for underserved populations. By investing in financial inclusion, impact investors can help to reduce poverty and promote economic growth.

- ***Healthcare***

Impact investing can support healthcare by investing in companies that are developing innovative healthcare solutions, improving access to healthcare services, and promoting healthy lifestyles. By investing in healthcare, impact investors can help to improve public health and well-being.

# CHAPTER TWO

**Understanding Social and Environmental Goals of impact investment**

Impact investing aims to generate positive social and environmental outcomes alongside financial returns. To achieve these goals, impact investors focus on investing in companies and projects that are aligned with their social and environmental values. The social goals of impact investing can encompass a broad range of issues, including:

- *Economic development*

Impact investors may seek to support companies and projects that promote economic development by creating jobs, supporting small businesses, and providing access to finance for underserved communities.

- *Education*

Impact investors may seek to support companies and projects that promote access to education, such as those developing educational technology or providing education and training for marginalized communities.

- *Healthcare*

Impact investors may seek to support companies and projects that improve healthcare access and quality, such as those developing innovative medical technologies or providing healthcare services to underserved populations.

- *Social justice*

Impact investors may seek to support companies and projects that promote social justice, such as those working to address income inequality, promote gender and racial equity, or support immigrant rights.

The environmental goals of impact investing can also encompass a broad range of issues, including:

- ***Climate change***

Impact investors may seek to support companies and projects that reduce greenhouse gas emissions, develop renewable energy sources, improve energy efficiency, or promote sustainable transportation.

- ***Sustainable agriculture***

Impact investors may seek to support companies and projects that promote sustainable agriculture practices, such as regenerative farming, reducing food waste, and increasing access to healthy food.

- ***Conservation***

Impact investors may seek to support companies and projects that promote the conservation of natural resources, such as those working to protect forests, oceans, and other natural ecosystems.

- ***Waste reduction***

Impact investors may seek to support companies and projects that reduce waste and promote circular economy practices, such as those developing innovative recycling technologies or promoting sustainable packaging solutions.

By aligning their investments with their social and environmental values, impact investors can play a vital role in driving positive social and environmental outcomes. They can also leverage their investment capital to encourage companies to adopt more sustainable and socially responsible business practices, which can lead to broader systemic change.

**Defining Social and Environmental Goals**

Defining social and environmental goals is an essential aspect of impact investing. Social and environmental goals are specific outcomes that investors seek to achieve through their investments, in addition to financial returns. Social goals may include issues related to economic development, education, healthcare, social justice, and more. For example, an investor may seek to invest in companies that promote economic development in underserved communities by creating jobs, supporting small businesses, and providing access to finance.

Environmental goals may include issues related to climate change, sustainable agriculture, conservation, and waste reduction. For example, an investor may seek to invest in companies that reduce greenhouse gas emissions, develop renewable energy sources, or promote sustainable agriculture practices.

Defining social and environmental goals is essential to ensure that impact investments are aligned with the investor's values and mission. It helps investors to identify investment opportunities that are more likely to generate positive social and environmental outcomes and avoid investments that may have negative social or environmental impacts.

Defining social and environmental goals can also help investors to measure and track the impact of their investments. By setting specific, measurable, and time-bound goals, investors can evaluate the success of their investments in achieving the desired social and environmental outcomes. This can provide investors with valuable insights into the effectiveness of their investment strategies and help them to refine their approach over time.

Overall, defining social and environmental goals is a crucial step in impact investing. It enables investors to align their investments with their values, identify impactful investment opportunities, and measure and track the impact of their investments. By doing so, investors can achieve their financial goals while also generating positive social and environmental outcomes.

## Identifying Social and Environmental Issues

Identifying social and environmental issues is a critical aspect of impact investing. Impact investors seek to invest in companies or projects that address specific social and environmental challenges. Therefore, it is essential to identify these challenges and understand their underlying causes to develop effective investment strategies. Once investors have identified social and environmental issues, they can develop investment strategies that target these challenges. For example, an investor interested in promoting sustainable agriculture may seek to invest in companies that promote regenerative farming practices, reduce food waste, or increase access to healthy food. There are many ways to identify social and environmental issues. Here are a few examples:

- ***Research***

Impact investors can conduct research to identify social and environmental issues that align with their values and mission. They can use various resources, such as academic research, industry reports, and news articles, to identify issues that are relevant to their investment objectives.

- ***Community engagement***

Impact investors can engage with communities and stakeholders to understand their specific social and environmental challenges. This can involve attending community meetings, conducting interviews with local leaders, and collaborating with organizations that work on the ground to address social and environmental issues.

- ***Impact measurement***

Impact investors can use impact measurement tools to identify social and environmental issues and track their progress over time. These tools can help investors to identify specific areas where they can make a difference and allocate their resources effectively.

- ***Industry expertise***

Impact investors may also leverage their industry expertise to identify social and environmental issues. For example, a healthcare expert may identify access to healthcare as a critical social issue, while a renewable energy expert may focus on reducing carbon emissions.

## Measuring Social and Environmental Impact

Measuring social and environmental impact is a critical aspect of impact investing. Measuring social and environmental impact is not always easy, and it can require significant resources and expertise. It enables investors to evaluate the effectiveness of their investments and contribute to a more sustainable and equitable world. By measuring social and environmental impact, impact investors can ensure that their investments are aligned with their values and generate positive outcomes for society and the environment.

Impact investors seek to generate positive social and environmental outcomes, in addition to financial returns. Therefore, it is essential to measure the impact of investments to understand their effectiveness and identify areas for improvement. Here are some approaches to measuring social and environmental impact:

- ***Metrics***

Impact investors can use metrics to measure social and environmental impact. These metrics can include both quantitative and qualitative data, such as the number of jobs created, carbon emissions reduced, or the percentage of the population served by a particular program.

- ***Standards and frameworks***

Impact investors may also use standards and frameworks, such as the Global Reporting Initiative (GRI) or the United Nations Sustainable Development Goals (SDGs), to guide their impact measurement efforts. These frameworks provide guidelines for measuring and reporting social and environmental impact, making it easier for investors to compare the impact of their investments over time.

- ***Impact assessments***

Impact investors can conduct impact assessments to evaluate the effectiveness of their investments. These assessments can involve surveys, interviews, or focus groups to gather data on the social and environmental outcomes of investments. Impact assessments can provide valuable insights into the effectiveness of investment strategies and identify areas for improvement.

- ***Third-party verification***

Impact investors may also seek third-party verification of their impact. This can involve engaging independent evaluators or certification bodies to assess the social and environmental impact of investments. Third-party verification can provide investors with credible and objective data on the impact of their investments, enhancing their credibility and transparency.

## Risks and Challenges of Impact Investing

Impact investing has gained popularity in recent years due to its potential to generate financial returns while also creating positive social and environmental outcomes.

However, like any investment strategy, impact investing also involves risks and challenges. Here are some of the risks and challenges associated with impact investing:

- ***Limited investment opportunities***

Impact investing is still a relatively new field, and there may be limited investment opportunities that align with an investor's values and mission. This can make it difficult to find suitable investments that generate both financial and social returns.

- ***Impact measurement challenges***

Measuring the social and environmental impact of investments can be challenging, particularly for small and early-stage companies. Investors may also face difficulties in agreeing on common metrics and standards for measuring impact, making it difficult to compare the impact of different investments.

- *Financial returns*

While impact investing seeks to generate both financial and social returns, there is a risk that investments may not achieve the desired financial returns. This can be due to market fluctuations, changes in consumer preferences, or other factors that affect the financial performance of investments.

- *Regulatory and legal risks*

Impact investing is subject to regulatory and legal risks, particularly in emerging markets where regulations may be unclear or inconsistent. Investors may also face reputational risks if their investments are associated with negative social or environmental outcomes.

- ***Ethical considerations***

Impact investors must navigate ethical considerations related to their investments, such as the potential for unintended consequences or conflicts of interest. For example, an investor may invest in a company that addresses climate change but may also be involved in activities that contribute to environmental degradation.

- ***Exit strategy***

Impact investments may be difficult to exit, particularly in cases where the company's social or environmental impact is integral to its operations. This can make it challenging for investors to realize returns on their investments.

Despite these risks and challenges, impact investing remains a promising investment strategy that can create positive social and environmental outcomes while also generating financial returns. To mitigate risks, investors can conduct thorough due diligence, work with experienced investment managers, and engage with stakeholders to ensure that investments align with their values and mission. By doing so, investors can achieve their financial objectives while also contributing to a more sustainable and equitable world.

**Financial Goals and Returns of Impact Investing**

Financial goals and returns are critical aspects of impact investing. Impact investors seek to generate both social and environmental benefits, but also aim to achieve financial returns that are commensurate with the risk of the investment. Investors should establish clear financial objectives, evaluate the risks and returns of potential investments, and diversify their impact investment portfolio. With careful evaluation and planning, impact investing can provide a viable investment strategy for those seeking to achieve both financial and social/environmental objectives. Here are some key points to consider when evaluating the financial goals and returns of impact investing:

- *Financial objectives*

Like traditional investing, impact investing seeks to generate financial returns that meet or exceed the investor's expectations. Investors may have different financial goals, such as capital preservation, income generation, or long-term capital growth. It is important to establish clear financial objectives before making an impact investment.

- ***Risk and return trade-off***

Impact investments, like any other investment, involve risks. Investors must evaluate the risks associated with a potential investment and assess whether the potential returns are commensurate with the risk. Higher-risk investments may offer higher potential returns, but they also carry a greater risk of loss.

- ***Impact on financial returns***

The social and environmental goals of impact investing may affect financial returns. For example, investing in a company that prioritizes sustainable practices may require higher upfront costs, which may reduce short-term financial returns. However, such investments may have long-term financial benefits, such as improved brand reputation or reduced operating costs.

- ***Diversification***

Diversification is essential in any investment portfolio, including impact investments. Investing in a variety of sectors, geographies, and types of investments can help to mitigate risk and enhance potential returns.

- ***Exit strategy***

Investors should consider their exit strategy before making an impact investment. An exit strategy is a plan for how and when to sell an investment. Some impact investments may have longer holding periods, making them less liquid than traditional investments. Investors should consider their liquidity needs and the potential exit options for their impact investments.

# CHAPTER THREE

**Investment Strategies for Aligning Financial Goals with Social and Environmental Goals**

Investment strategies for aligning financial goals with social and environmental goals are becoming increasingly popular as investors seek to generate returns while making a positive impact on the world. Here are a few investment strategies that can help investors align their financial goals with their social and environmental goals:

- ***Environmental, Social, and Governance (ESG) Integration***

ESG Integration refers to the practice of incorporating environmental, social, and governance (ESG) factors into investment decision-making processes. ESG Integration has become an increasingly popular approach to investing in recent years, as investors recognize that non-financial factors can have a significant impact on a company's long-term financial performance and sustainability. By considering ESG factors, investors can identify companies that are more likely to have sustainable business models, strong corporate governance practices, and positive social and environmental impact. By integrating ESG factors into their investment analysis, investors can gain a more comprehensive view of a company's risks and opportunities and make more informed investment decisions.

- ***Impact Investing***

Impact investing involves investing in companies or organizations that are dedicated to creating positive social or environmental impact. These investments are often made in areas such as renewable energy, affordable housing, education, healthcare, and other impact-driven initiatives. Impact investors seek to achieve both financial returns and measurable social or environmental impact.

- ***Community Investing***

Community investing involves investing in organizations that provide financial services and support to underserved communities. These investments may include community development banks, credit unions, or microfinance institutions. Community investors seek to generate financial returns while supporting economic development and social equity in underserved communities.

- ***Shareholder Advocacy***

Shareholder advocacy involves using shareholder voting rights and engagement to influence corporate behavior on social and environmental issues. Shareholders may file resolutions or engage in dialogue with companies to encourage them to improve their practices on issues such as climate change, human rights, or board diversity.

- ***Sustainable Investing***

Sustainable investing is a broad category of investment strategies that incorporate environmental, social, and governance factors into investment decision-making processes. Sustainable investors seek to identify companies that are best positioned to generate long-term returns by managing ESG risks and opportunities effectively.

- ***Green Bonds***

Green bonds are fixed-income securities that are used to finance environmentally beneficial projects, such as renewable energy or energy efficiency initiatives. Investors who purchase green bonds can earn a fixed income while supporting a positive environmental impact.

- ***Social Bonds***

Social bonds are similar to green bonds but are used to finance social initiatives, such as affordable housing or healthcare projects. Investors who purchase social bonds can earn a fixed income while supporting a positive social impact.

- ***Thematic Investing***

Thematic investing involves identifying long-term macroeconomic trends and themes that have the potential to drive growth and generate a positive impact. Thematic investing is a strategy that involves investing in companies that are aligned with specific social or environmental themes, such as clean energy, water scarcity, or gender equality. This approach seeks to identify companies that are poised to benefit from trends and innovations that address global challenges.

- ***Divestment***

Divestment involves selling investments in companies or industries that are deemed harmful to the environment or society, such as fossil fuels or tobacco. Divestment can send a powerful signal to companies and policymakers that investors are concerned about social and environmental issues and can be used to encourage positive change.

- ***Corporate Engagement***

This strategy involves using shareholder advocacy, proxy voting, and other forms of engagement to influence company behavior on ESG issues. This approach can involve working with companies to adopt and implement policies and practices that prioritize environmental sustainability, social responsibility, and good corporate governance.

- ***Community Investing***

Community investing involves investing in organizations and funds that support economic development and social equity in underserved communities. This approach can include community development banks, credit unions, or microfinance institutions.

# CHAPTER FOUR

**Measuring the Impact of Impact Investing**

Measuring the impact of impact investing is an essential part of the investment process. Impact investors seek to generate positive social and environmental outcomes alongside financial returns, and measuring the impact of these investments is crucial for evaluating their effectiveness and ensuring accountability to stakeholders.

Measuring the impact of impact investing requires a multifaceted approach that takes into account both quantitative and qualitative data, distinguishes between outputs and outcomes, carefully considers attribution, and emphasizes transparency and reporting. While impact measurement can be challenging, it is a crucial part of impact investing and helps ensure that investments are generating positive social and environmental outcomes alongside financial returns. Here are some of the key methods used to measure the impact of impact investing:

- ***Impact frameworks and standards***

Impact investors use various frameworks and standards to measure the social and environmental impact of their investments. These frameworks and standards provide guidelines for defining impact, setting targets, and measuring progress. Examples of impact frameworks and standards include the United Nations' Sustainable Development Goals (SDGs), the Global Impact Investing Network (GIIN) Impact Reporting and Investment Standards (IRIS), and the Social Return on Investment (SROI) methodology.

- ***Metrics and indicators***

Impact investors use a range of metrics and indicators to measure the impact of their investments. These metrics and indicators can vary depending on the type of investment and the desired outcomes. For example, metrics for renewable energy investments might include the amount of carbon emissions reduced, while metrics for investments in affordable housing might include the number of families housed.

- ***Impact reports***

Impact investors produce impact reports to document the social and environmental impact of their investments. Impact reports provide transparency to investors and stakeholders and help track progress toward achieving impact goals. These reports can include data on the number of people served, the amount of carbon emissions reduced, and other metrics that demonstrate the impact of the investment.

- ***Third-party evaluations***

Impact investors can also commission third-party evaluations to assess the impact of their investments. These evaluations provide an independent assessment of the social and environmental outcomes of the investment and can help identify areas for improvement.

- ***Qualitative versus quantitative data***

Impact investors often use a combination of qualitative and quantitative data to measure impact. Qualitative data can help provide a deeper understanding of the social and environmental context in which an investment operates, while quantitative data provides more concrete metrics for measuring impact. For example, while a qualitative assessment might describe the positive impact of a healthcare investment on the well-being of patients and their families, quantitative data could be used to measure the number of patients served, the reduction in hospital readmissions, and other concrete outcomes.

- ***Outcomes versus outputs***

Impact investors distinguish between outputs (what an investment produces) and outcomes (the broader social and environmental impacts of an investment). While outputs can be measured using quantitative data, outcomes are often more difficult to measure and require a more nuanced approach. For example, an investment in a renewable energy project might produce a specific amount of clean energy, but its broader impact on reducing carbon emissions would be considered an outcome.

- ***Attribution***

Measuring the impact of impact investing requires careful consideration of the role that the investment played in achieving positive social and environmental outcomes. While it can be difficult to attribute impact to a specific investment, impact investors often use a range of techniques to identify the contribution of their investments to positive outcomes. These techniques can include counterfactual analysis, which compares the outcomes of an investment to what would have happened in the absence of the investment, and stakeholder analysis, which seeks to understand the perspectives of different stakeholders affected by an investment.

- ***Reporting and transparency***
Impact investors are increasingly expected to report on the social and environmental impact of their investments in a transparent and accessible manner. This requires clear communication of impact metrics, including how they were measured and any limitations or uncertainties associated with the data. In addition to impact reports, impact investors may also use other methods to communicate impact to stakeholders, such as case studies, impact stories, and interactive dashboards.

## Risks and Challenges of Impact Investing

Like any investment strategy, impact investing comes with a range of risks and challenges, including challenges related to impact measurement, limited investment opportunities, financial returns, market volatility, lack of regulation, impact washing, ethical considerations, scalability, limited exit options, market and political instability, cost and complexity of due diligence, limited data and standardization, lack of awareness and understanding, and complexity of social and environmental challenges. Here are some of the key risks and challenges to consider when engaging in impact investing:

- ***Impact measurement***

Measuring the impact of impact investments can be challenging, particularly for investments with long-term outcomes or indirect impacts. This can make it difficult to evaluate the effectiveness of an investment and to demonstrate its impact to stakeholders.

- ***Limited investment opportunities***

Impact investing is a relatively new field, and as such, there may be a limited number of investment opportunities available in certain areas or sectors. This can make it challenging to achieve diversification and allocate capital effectively.

- ***Financial returns***

While impact investors aim to generate both financial returns and positive social and environmental outcomes, there may be trade-offs between the two. Impact investments may offer lower financial returns than traditional investments, particularly in the short term, which can make them less attractive to some investors.

- ***Market volatility***

Impact investments may be more vulnerable to market volatility than traditional investments, particularly in emerging markets or in sectors with less established track records. This can make it difficult to predict returns and manage risk effectively.

- ***Lack of regulation***

The impact investing field is not yet subject to a standardized regulatory framework, which can create uncertainty and confusion for investors. This can make it difficult to evaluate investment opportunities and ensure that investments are aligned with the desired social and environmental outcomes.

- ***Impact washing***

There is a risk that some investments marketed as impact investments may not deliver on their promised social and environmental outcomes. This can be due to a lack of robust impact measurement and reporting, or to intentional misrepresentation by investment managers.

- ***Ethical considerations***

Impact investors must navigate a range of ethical considerations, including balancing the desired social and environmental outcomes with the interests of all stakeholders, and avoiding investments that may have negative impacts on certain groups or communities.

- ***Scalability***

Many impact investments are designed to operate on a small scale, and it can be challenging to scale up successful investments to achieve a broader impact.

This can limit the ability of impact investors to achieve large-scale social and environmental change.

- ***Limited exit options***

Impact investments may have limited exit options, particularly in cases where investments are made in small and medium-sized enterprises or developing countries. This can make it difficult to achieve liquidity and realize returns on investment.

- ***Market and political instability***

Impact investments can be particularly vulnerable to market and political instability, particularly in developing countries or in areas affected by conflict or instability. This can make it difficult to predict returns and manage risk effectively.

- ***Cost and complexity of due diligence***

Impact investors often face higher costs and greater complexity in conducting due diligence on potential investments, particularly in cases where investments are made in less developed regions or sectors. This can make it challenging to identify high-quality investment opportunities and manage risk effectively.

- ***Limited data and standardization***

Impact investing is still a relatively new field, and as such, there is limited data and standardization around impact metrics and reporting. This can make it challenging to compare the impact of different investments and to identify best practices.

- ***Lack of awareness and understanding***

Many investors are still unfamiliar with impact investing and may not understand the potential benefits or risks of investing in social and environmental causes. This can make it challenging to raise capital for impact investments and to grow the impact investing field more broadly.

- ***The complexity of social and environmental challenges***

Many of the social and environmental challenges that impact investors seek to address are complex and multifaceted, and may require systemic change rather than individual investments. This can make it challenging to achieve measurable impact through investment alone.

## Balancing Financial Returns with Social and Environmental Impact

Balancing financial returns with social and environmental impact is a central challenge of impact investing. It requires careful consideration of impact objectives, impact measurement, financial risk, diversification, complementary strategies, patience, and transparent communication. Impact investors seek to generate both financial returns and positive social and environmental outcomes, but there may be trade-offs between the two. Here are some key considerations for balancing financial returns with social and environmental impact:

- ***Define impact objectives***

Impact investors should clearly define their social and environmental impact objectives, and prioritize them based on their importance. This can help ensure that investments are aligned with desired impact outcomes.

- ***Consider impact measurement***

Impact measurement is critical for evaluating the effectiveness of impact investments and balancing financial returns with social and environmental impact. Impact investors should develop clear impact metrics and reporting mechanisms to track the impact of their investments over time.

- ***Evaluate financial risk***

Impact investors must also evaluate financial risk alongside social and environmental impact. This requires assessing the financial risks associated with each investment and balancing them against the potential social and environmental benefits.

- ***Seek diversification***

Diversification is important for managing risk and balancing financial returns with social and environmental impact. Impact investors should seek to diversify their portfolios across different impact areas, geographies, and investment types.

- ***Identify complementary strategies***

Impact investors can also identify complementary strategies to balance financial returns with social and environmental impact. For example, impact investors may seek to influence companies through shareholder advocacy, or invest in social enterprises that generate both financial returns and social impact.

- ***Be patient***

Impact investments often require a longer time horizon than traditional investments, and may generate lower financial returns in the short term. Impact investors should be patient and focus on the long-term potential of their investments to achieve both financial and impact objectives.

- ***Communicate transparently***

Finally, impact investors should communicate transparently with stakeholders about their financial and impact objectives, investment strategies, and impact measurement and reporting. This can help build trust and credibility with stakeholders and demonstrate a commitment to balancing financial returns with social and environmental impact.

- ***Emphasize impact as a driver of financial returns***

Impact investors can focus on investments that align with their impact objectives and have the potential to generate strong financial returns. Research has shown that investments with strong environmental and social performance can deliver competitive financial returns, as companies that prioritize sustainability and social impact are often well-managed and well-positioned for long-term success.

- ***Incorporate environmental, social, and governance (ESG) factors***

Incorporating ESG factors into investment analysis and decision-making can help investors identify and assess both financial and impact risks and opportunities. By considering factors such as climate change, social impact, and governance practices, investors can gain a more holistic view of investment opportunities and their potential to generate financial and impact returns.

- **Seek out impact-aligned investment opportunities**

Investors can seek out investment opportunities that are specifically designed to achieve both financial and impact objectives. For example, impact investing funds may focus on specific impact themes, such as clean energy, affordable housing, or sustainable agriculture. These investments can offer investors a way to target specific impact outcomes while also generating financial returns.

- ***Develop impact measurement and reporting frameworks***

Impact investors can develop clear and consistent impact measurement and reporting frameworks to track the social and environmental outcomes of their investments. These frameworks can help investors assess the effectiveness of their investments in achieving impact objectives and make informed decisions about future investments.

- ***Engage with companies***

Investors can engage with companies to encourage them to improve their environmental, social, and governance practices. This can include advocating for stronger sustainability policies, engaging with management teams to address impact risks and opportunities, and voting in favor of shareholder resolutions that align with impact objectives.

- ***Consider the broader impact ecosystem***

Impact investors can consider the broader impact ecosystem, including policy frameworks, market infrastructure, and stakeholder engagement when seeking to achieve both financial and impact objectives. By working with other investors, policymakers, and stakeholders, investors can help build a more supportive ecosystem for impact investing and advance positive social and environmental outcomes.

**Impact Investing in Practice**

Impact investing is the practice of investing in companies, organizations, or funds to generate positive social and environmental impact alongside a financial return. In practice, impact investing can take many forms and can be implemented by a range of investors, from individual investors to large institutions. Here are some ways that impact investing is put into practice:

- ***Direct investments***

One way to practice impact investing is to make direct investments in companies or organizations that have a mission or business model aligned with your impact goals. This can involve investing in early-stage startups that are developing innovative solutions to social or environmental challenges or investing in established companies that have a track record of delivering positive impact.

- ***Private equity and venture capital***

Private equity and venture capital funds are investment vehicles that pool capital from investors to make investments in private companies. Many impact investing funds are structured as private equity or venture capital funds, which can provide opportunities for investors to achieve both financial returns and social or environmental impact.

- *Public equities*

Another way to practice impact investing is to invest in public equities, such as stocks or bonds, of companies that are committed to generating positive social and environmental impact. This can involve investing in companies that are leaders in sustainability or that have a positive impact on their local communities.

- *Community investing*

Community investing involves investing in projects or organizations that have a direct impact on underserved or disadvantaged communities. This can involve investing in community development financial institutions (CDFIs) that provide financing to small businesses and affordable housing projects or investing in social enterprises that create jobs and economic opportunities in low-income areas.

- ***ESG integration***

ESG integration is the practice of incorporating environmental, social, and governance (ESG) factors into investment decision-making. This can involve analyzing a company's ESG performance and using that information to inform investment decisions. Many impact investors use ESG integration as a way to identify companies that are aligned with their impact goals.

- ***Impact-focused funds***

Impact-focused funds are investment vehicles that are specifically designed to generate positive social and environmental impact alongside a financial return. These funds can be structured as mutual funds, exchange-traded funds (ETFs), or other investment vehicles.

- ***Impact measurement and management***

Impact investors often work to measure and manage the social and environmental impact of their investments. This can involve setting impact targets, monitoring progress towards those targets, and reporting on impact outcomes. There are a variety of impact measurement frameworks and tools available, including the Impact Management Project and the Global Impact Investing Network's IRIS+ system.

- ***Collaborative initiatives***

Impact investors often collaborate with other investors, governments, and nonprofits to maximize their impact. This can involve joining collaborative initiatives such as the Sustainable Development Goals (SDGs) or participating in impact-focused networks such as the Impact Investing Alliance.

- ***Advocacy and policy engagement***

Impact investors may also engage in advocacy and policy efforts to support positive social and environmental outcomes. This can involve advocating for policies that support impact investing or engaging with policymakers to help shape regulations and policy frameworks that enable impact investing.

- ***Blended finance***

Blended finance is the use of public or philanthropic capital to mobilize private investment toward social and environmental objectives. Impact investors may leverage blended finance structures to increase the impact of their investments and create more scalable solutions to social and environmental challenges.

- ***Impact bonds***

Impact bonds are a type of performance-based financing mechanism in which investors provide capital to fund social or environmental programs, and receive a return based on the achievement of pre-determined outcomes. Impact investors may invest in impact bonds as a way to align their financial returns with positive social and environmental outcomes.

## Impact Investing and the Role of Business in Society

Impact investing is closely linked to the role of business in society, as it seeks to harness the power of business to address social and environmental challenges. By doing so, impact investing can help to create a more sustainable and equitable world while generating financial returns for investors. Here are some ways that impact investing relates to the role of business in society:

- *Creating shared value*

Impact investing seeks to create shared value, or economic value that also creates social and environmental value. By investing in companies and organizations that are creating positive social and environmental outcomes, impact investors are helping to demonstrate the business case for creating shared value.

- ***Encouraging corporate social responsibility***

Impact investing can encourage companies to take social and environmental issues seriously by demonstrating that there is a financial case for doing so. Companies that prioritize social and environmental outcomes may be more attractive to impact investors, which can provide a financial incentive for companies to incorporate social and environmental considerations into their business practices.

- ***Advancing the Sustainable Development Goals***

The Sustainable Development Goals (SDGs) are a set of 17 goals established by the United Nations to address social and environmental challenges. Impact investing can play a key role in advancing the SDGs by providing capital to support companies and organizations that are working towards these goals.

- ***Supporting inclusive economic growth***

Impact investing can help to support inclusive economic growth by providing capital to businesses and organizations that are focused on creating positive social and environmental outcomes. By supporting these types of businesses, impact investors can help to create jobs and promote economic development in underserved communities.

- ***Fostering innovation***

Impact investing can also help to foster innovation by providing capital to businesses and organizations that are focused on developing new solutions to social and environmental challenges. By supporting innovative solutions, impact investors can help to drive progress towards a more sustainable and equitable world.

- ***Encouraging stakeholder capitalism***

Impact investing can encourage businesses to adopt a more stakeholder-centric approach, which recognizes that the interests of all stakeholders, including employees, customers, suppliers, and communities, are important. By investing in businesses that prioritize social and environmental outcomes, impact investors can help to support a more stakeholder-centric approach to business.

- ***Driving accountability***

Impact investing can help to drive accountability by encouraging businesses to be transparent about their social and environmental impacts. Impact investors may require companies to report on their social and environmental performance, which can help to drive positive changes in business practices.

- ***Promoting sustainable business models***

Impact investing can help to promote sustainable business models by providing capital to businesses that are focused on creating positive social and environmental outcomes. By supporting these types of businesses, impact investors can help to drive innovation and promote a transition to more sustainable business practices.

- ***Addressing market failures***

Impact investing can help to address market failures by providing capital to businesses and organizations that are focused on addressing social and environmental challenges that may not be adequately addressed by traditional market forces. By doing so, impact investors can help to drive progress towards a more equitable and sustainable world.

- ***Fostering collaboration***

Impact investing can also help to foster collaboration between businesses, governments, and civil society organizations to address social and environmental challenges. By bringing together stakeholders from different sectors, impact investing can help to drive progress towards shared goals.

- ***Making a Difference through Impact Investing***

Impact investing can make a significant difference by promoting engagement with stakeholders, fostering transparency and accountability, encouraging responsible investment practices, supporting sustainable development, and promoting diversity and inclusion. It allows investors to support businesses and organizations that are working to address social and environmental challenges, while also generating financial returns.

By leveraging the power of finance to support social and environmental outcomes, impact investors can help to create a more sustainable and equitable future for all. Here are some ways that impact investing can make a difference:

- ***Addressing pressing social and environmental challenges***

Impact investing can provide critical funding to organizations that are working to address pressing social and environmental challenges, such as poverty, climate change, and inequality. By investing in these organizations, impact investors can help to accelerate progress towards a more sustainable and equitable future.

- ***Promoting innovation***

Impact investing can also promote innovation by providing capital to businesses and organizations that are developing new solutions to social and environmental challenges. By supporting these innovative ideas, impact investors can help to drive progress towards more sustainable and equitable systems.

- ***Supporting underserved communities***

Impact investing can also help to support underserved communities by providing funding to organizations that are working to address social and economic inequality. By investing in these organizations, impact investors can help to provide resources and opportunities to communities that may otherwise be overlooked.

- ***Creating positive financial returns***

Impact investing also offers the potential for positive financial returns, which can help to attract more capital to support social and environmental causes. By demonstrating that impact investing can generate competitive financial returns, investors can help to shift more capital towards organizations that are making a positive difference.

- ***Driving systemic change***

Impact investing can also help to drive systemic change by promoting more sustainable and equitable business practices. By investing in businesses that prioritize social and environmental outcomes, impact investors can help to encourage other businesses to adopt similar practices.

- ***Engaging with stakeholders***

Impact investing can promote engagement with stakeholders, including businesses, governments, civil society organizations, and communities. By collaborating with these stakeholders, impact investors can help to build partnerships and networks that can drive positive change.

- ***Fostering transparency and accountability***

Impact investing can also promote transparency and accountability by requiring organizations to report on their social and environmental impact. By holding these organizations accountable for their impact, impact investors can help to ensure that they are making a positive difference.

- ***Encouraging responsible investment practices***

Impact investing can also encourage responsible investment practices by promoting environmental, social, and governance (ESG) criteria. By investing in companies that meet these criteria, impact investors can encourage more responsible business practices and help to mitigate risks.

- ***Supporting sustainable development***

Impact investing can also support sustainable development by investing in projects that promote economic growth while also protecting the environment and supporting social inclusion. By investing in these projects, impact investors can help to promote long-term sustainable development and support the achievement of the United Nations' Sustainable Development Goals.

- ***Encouraging diversity and inclusion***

Impact investing can also promote diversity and inclusion by investing in businesses that prioritize these values. By investing in businesses that are committed to promoting diversity and inclusion, impact investors can help to create a more equitable and inclusive society.

# CHAPTER FIVE

**Overcoming Barriers to Impact Investing**

Impact investing, which involves investing in companies, organizations, or funds that aim to generate positive social or environmental impact alongside financial returns, is gaining momentum as a powerful tool for creating positive change in the world. However, there are still several barriers to impact investing that need to be overcome to make it more mainstream.

However, overcoming the barriers to impact investing requires a coordinated effort from all stakeholders involved, including investors, fund managers, policymakers, and impact measurement experts. By addressing these barriers, impact investing can become a mainstream approach to investing that generates both financial returns and positive social and environmental impact. In this response, I will broaden on the barriers and explore some of the ways they can be overcome:

- ***Lack of awareness and education***

A significant barrier to impact investing is the lack of awareness and education about its potential benefits. Many investors, particularly those who are more risk-averse, may not be familiar with the concept of impact investing, or may not understand how it differs from traditional investing. To overcome this barrier, there needs to be more education and awareness-raising about the potential benefits of impact investing, such as generating positive social and environmental impact, diversifying investment portfolios, and attracting millennial investors.

- ***Lack of investment opportunities***

Another barrier to impact investing is the lack of investment opportunities that meet the criteria for impact investing. Many impact investors have specific investment criteria that they use to evaluate potential investments, such as a focus on social or environmental impact, a clear measurement of impact, and a financial return. To overcome this barrier, there needs to be an increase in the number of investment opportunities that meet these criteria. This can be achieved by developing new impact-focused funds or working with existing fund managers to integrate impact criteria into their investment strategies.

- ***Limited financial returns***

Some investors may perceive impact investing as a trade-off between financial returns and social or environmental impact. However, evidence suggests that impact investments can generate competitive financial returns while also achieving social and environmental impact. To overcome this barrier, there needs to be more data and evidence to demonstrate the financial viability of impact investing. This can be achieved by conducting more rigorous impact assessments and reporting financial returns alongside social and environmental impact.

- ***Regulatory barriers***

Regulatory barriers can also prevent impact investing from becoming mainstream. For example, some regulatory frameworks may not be conducive to impact investing, or may not recognize the importance of social and environmental impact. To overcome this barrier, there needs to be greater awareness and understanding of the potential benefits of impact investing among regulators, and regulatory frameworks need to be adjusted to support impact investing. This can be achieved by engaging with policymakers and advocating for regulatory changes that encourage and support impact investing.

- ***Lack of measurement and standardization***

Finally, a key barrier to impact investing is the lack of measurement and standardization of impact metrics. Many impact investors have different metrics for measuring social and environmental impact, which can make it difficult to compare and evaluate investments. To overcome this barrier, there needs to be greater standardization of impact metrics and more robust measurement frameworks to evaluate the impact of impact investments. This can be achieved by developing industry-wide standards for impact measurement and evaluation, and by investing in research and development to improve impact assessment methodologies.

## Evaluating Impact Investing Opportunities

Evaluating impact investing opportunities can be a complex process due to the unique combination of financial and social or environmental impact considerations. In this response, I will elaborate on the steps for evaluating impact investing opportunities:

- **Define your impact goals**

The first step in evaluating impact investing opportunities is to define your impact goals. This involves identifying the social or environmental issues you want to address through your investment and the outcomes you hope to achieve. For example, your impact goals may include reducing carbon emissions, improving access to healthcare, or increasing financial inclusion. Defining your impact goals will help you focus your search for impact investment opportunities and ensure that you are investing in projects or companies that align with your values.

- ***Conduct research***

Once you have defined your impact goals, it's essential to research to identify potential impact investing opportunities. This can include reading industry reports, attending impact investing conferences, and networking with impact investors and fund managers. You can also use online platforms such as ImpactBase or the Global Impact Investing Network (GIIN) to search for impact investing opportunities. When conducting research, it's important to assess the quality of the information available and consider multiple sources to ensure a comprehensive understanding of the investment opportunity.

- ***Evaluate impact metrics***

Impact metrics are used to measure the social or environmental impact generated by an investment. When evaluating impact investing opportunities, it's crucial to assess the impact metrics used by the investment opportunity. Impact metrics should be specific, measurable, and relevant to your impact goals. For example, if your impact goal is to reduce carbon emissions, you may want to evaluate the investment opportunity's carbon footprint reduction metrics. It's also important to consider the quality of the data used to calculate impact metrics and the methodology used to assess impact.

- ***Assess financial returns***

While impact investing aims to generate positive social or environmental impact, financial returns are also essential. When evaluating impact investing opportunities, it's important to assess the investment opportunity's financial performance, including its historical returns, risk profile and projected financial returns. This involves reviewing financial statements, conducting financial modeling, and assessing the investment's market potential. It's important to ensure that the financial returns of the investment align with your financial objectives.

- ***Consider the management team***

The management team is a critical component of the success of impact investment. When evaluating impact investing opportunities, it's important to assess the experience, track record, and alignment with the impact goals of the management team. This includes reviewing the qualifications and expertise of the key members of the management team, their experience in managing similar investments, and their commitment to social and environmental impact.

- ***Evaluate the exit strategy***

Impact investments are often long-term investments, but it's essential to consider the exit strategy for the investment. This involves assessing the potential risks and returns of the exit strategy and understanding how the investment will be exited. The exit strategy can include options such as a sale to a strategic buyer, an IPO, or a merger. It's important to ensure that the exit strategy aligns with your financial and impact objectives.

- ***Assess the legal and regulatory environment***

Impact investing is subject to a range of legal and regulatory requirements, which can vary by country and investment type. When evaluating impact investing opportunities, it's essential to assess the legal and regulatory environment and ensure that the investment complies with all relevant laws and regulations. This includes reviewing the investment documents and assessing the risks associated with legal and regulatory compliance.

- ***Conduct due diligence***

Conducting due diligence is a crucial step in evaluating impact investing opportunities. This involves conducting a thorough review of the investment opportunity, including the company or organization's financial statements, impact metrics, management team, legal and regulatory compliance, and other relevant information. Due diligence should be conducted by a qualified team with expertise in impact investing and financial analysis.

- ***Monitor and measure the impact***

Once you have invested in an impact investment opportunity, it's important to monitor and measure its impact. This involves regularly reviewing the impact metrics and financial performance of the investment and assessing its progress toward achieving your impact goals. Monitoring and measuring impact can help you identify opportunities for improvement and ensure that your investment is generating the desired social or environmental impact.

## The Role of Impact Investing in a Sustainable Future

The role of impact investing in a sustainable future is critical. Impact investing provides a means for investors to generate financial returns while also driving positive social and environmental outcomes. By investing in initiatives that address global challenges, impact investors can contribute to a more sustainable future in several ways:

- ***Addressing pressing social and environmental challenges***

Impact investing enables investors to support initiatives that address pressing social and environmental challenges, such as poverty, climate change, and inequality. By directing capital towards these issues, impact investors can help to drive positive social and environmental outcomes.

- ***Unlocking new sources of funding***

Impact investing has the potential to unlock new sources of funding for social and environmental initiatives. By attracting private sector investment, impact investing can complement public sector financing, philanthropic funding, and other sources of capital, increasing the overall amount of funding available for sustainable development.

- ***Creating sustainable financial returns***

Impact investing can generate sustainable financial returns by investing in initiatives that create long-term value. By focusing on sustainability and impact, impact investors can identify investment opportunities that are well-positioned to generate financial returns over the long term.

- ***Influencing corporate behavior***
Impact investors can use their investments to influence corporate behavior and encourage companies to adopt more sustainable business practices. By investing in companies that prioritize environmental and social responsibility, impact investors can incentivize other companies to do the same.

- ***Promoting innovation***
Impact investing can promote innovation by investing in early-stage companies and start-ups that are developing new solutions to social and environmental challenges. By providing capital to these innovators, impact investors can help to drive technological and social innovation, leading to a more sustainable future.

- *Aligning financial and social objectives*

Impact investing enables investors to align their financial and social objectives. By investing in initiatives that generate positive social and environmental outcomes, impact investors can create financial value while also contributing to the achievement of global sustainable development goals.

- *Encouraging systemic change*

Impact investing can promote systemic change by investing in initiatives that drive sustainable development. This includes investments in renewable energy, sustainable agriculture, and affordable housing. By directing capital towards initiatives that drive systemic change, impact investors can help to accelerate the transition towards a more sustainable future.

- ***Building resilience***

Impact investing can help build resilience in the face of global challenges such as climate change, natural disasters, and pandemics. By investing in initiatives that build resilience, such as disaster relief, healthcare systems, and food security, impact investors can help communities to withstand shocks and build a more sustainable future.

- ***Engaging stakeholders***

Impact investing can engage stakeholders, including communities, civil society, and other stakeholders, in sustainable development initiatives. By involving stakeholders in the investment process, impact investors can ensure that investments are aligned with the needs and priorities of the communities they seek to serve.

- ***Supporting the SDGs***

Impact investing can support the achievement of the United Nations Sustainable Development Goals (SDGs) by investing in initiatives that align with the SDGs. The SDGs provide a framework for sustainable development, and impact investors can use them to identify investment opportunities that align with global development priorities.

- ***Creating shared value***

Impact investing can create shared value by investing in initiatives that generate social and environmental outcomes alongside financial returns. By creating shared value, impact investors can generate positive impacts for society while also creating value for their investors.

- ***Driving accountability and transparency***

Impact investing can drive accountability and transparency by establishing impact measurement and reporting frameworks. By measuring and reporting on social and environmental outcomes, impact investors can hold themselves accountable for the impacts of their investments and provide transparency to their investors and other stakeholders.

- ***Emerging Trends and Innovations***

Emerging trends and innovations are shaping the landscape of impact investing and providing new opportunities to generate positive social and environmental impact. In this response, I will elaborate on some of the emerging trends and innovations in impact investing.

- ***Sustainable Development Goals (SDGs)***

The United Nations' Sustainable Development Goals (SDGs) have emerged as a framework for measuring and achieving positive social and environmental impact. The SDGs are a set of 17 goals and 169 targets that aim to end poverty, protect the planet, and ensure prosperity for all. Impact investors are increasingly using the SDGs as a framework for evaluating and measuring impact.

- ***Impact-focused investment vehicles***

Impact-focused investment vehicles, such as social impact bonds, green bonds, and development impact bonds, have emerged as a way to channel capital toward specific social and environmental outcomes. These vehicles are designed to generate both financial returns and positive social or environmental impact.

- ***Technology-enabled impact investing***
Technology is playing an increasingly important role in impact investing, enabling investors to track and measure impact more effectively. Blockchain technology, for example, can provide transparency and traceability in supply chains, while artificial intelligence (AI) can help analyze impact metrics and identify investment opportunities.

- ***Diversity, equity, and inclusion (DEI)***
DEI has emerged as a critical consideration in impact investing, with investors recognizing the importance of investing in

companies and organizations that promote diversity, equity, and inclusion. This involves investing in companies that prioritize workplace diversity, social inclusion, and environmental justice.

- *Climate-focused investing*

Climate change is one of the most pressing global issues, and impact investors are increasingly focusing on investing in companies and organizations that are addressing this challenge. Climate-focused investing can include investing in renewable energy, energy efficiency, and sustainable agriculture.

- *Impact measurement and management*

Impact measurement and management (IMM) have emerged as a critical component of impact investing, providing a framework for assessing and managing impact. IMM involves defining impact goals, identifying impact metrics, and measuring and managing impact over time. There is an increasing focus on standardizing impact measurement and management to enable investors to compare and evaluate impact across different investments.

- ***Community investing***

Community investing involves investing in underserved communities, such as low-income neighborhoods and rural areas. Community investing can provide capital to small businesses, affordable housing projects, and community development initiatives, helping to promote economic development and social equity.

- ***Blended finance***

Blended finance involves combining public and private capital to finance social and environmental projects. This can involve using public funding to leverage private investment, reducing the risk for private investors, and increasing the scale of impact. Blended finance can be used to fund a wide range of projects, including sustainable infrastructure, education, and healthcare.

- ***Impact investing in emerging markets***

Impact investors are increasingly looking to emerging markets as a source of high-impact investment opportunities. Emerging markets offer opportunities for impact investors to invest in innovative solutions to social and environmental challenges, while also generating financial returns. However, investing in emerging markets can present unique challenges, such as political instability, weak legal systems, and currency risks.

- ***Philanthropic impact investing***

Philanthropic impact investing involves using philanthropic capital to generate social and environmental impact. This can involve making investments in social enterprises or funding impact-focused investment vehicles. Philanthropic impact investing can be used to address a wide range of social and environmental issues, including poverty, education, and healthcare.

- ***ESG investing***

ESG (Environmental, Social, and Governance) investing involves investing in companies that prioritize environmental and social responsibility and have strong governance practices. ESG investing has gained traction in recent years, with investors recognizing the importance of investing in companies that are aligned with their values and have a positive impact on society and the environment.

- ***Impact investing in education***

Education is a critical driver of social and economic development, and impact investors are increasingly investing in education-focused initiatives. This can involve investing in education technology (EdTech) startups, funding school infrastructure projects, or supporting education-focused non-profit organizations.

- ***Gender-lens investing***

Gender-lens investing involves investing in companies that prioritize gender equality and women's empowerment. This can involve investing in companies that have a strong track record of promoting gender diversity in the workplace, supporting women-led businesses, or addressing gender-specific challenges, such as maternal health.

- ***Impact investing in healthcare***

Healthcare is another critical area for impact investing, with investors recognizing the importance of investing in solutions that promote access to quality healthcare, particularly in underserved communities. This can involve investing in healthcare infrastructure, funding medical research, or supporting healthcare-focused non-profit organizations.

- ***Scaling Impact Investing Globally***

Scaling impact investing globally is critical for achieving the United Nations' Sustainable Development Goals (SDGs) and creating a more sustainable future. Impact investing can be a powerful tool for addressing global challenges, including poverty, climate change, and inequality. However, to achieve impact at scale, impact investors must overcome several challenges.

- ***Awareness***

One of the biggest challenges to scaling impact investing globally is raising awareness about its potential benefits. Many investors are not aware of the opportunities that impact investing presents, and there is a need for greater education and awareness-raising initiatives.

- ***Capacity building***

To scale impact investing, there is a need for capacity-building initiatives that help investors develop the necessary skills and knowledge to identify and evaluate impact investments. This includes training programs, mentorship opportunities, and networking initiatives.

- ***Standardization***

There is a need for standardized impact measurement and reporting frameworks to facilitate the comparison of impact investments across different regions and asset classes. Standardization can help to increase transparency and accountability, making it easier for investors to evaluate the social and environmental impact of their investments.

- *Collaboration*

To scale impact investing globally, there is a need for collaboration between investors, governments, civil society, and other stakeholders. Collaboration can help to align interests, leverage resources, and share best practices, leading to more effective and efficient impact investing initiatives.

- *Innovation*

Scaling impact investing globally requires innovation in investment structures, financial products, and impact measurement methodologies. New financial products, such as green bonds and social impact bonds, are already gaining traction, and there is a need for continued innovation to address emerging social and environmental challenges.

- ***Policy support***
Governments can play a critical role in scaling impact investing globally by providing policy support, such as tax incentives, regulatory frameworks, and public-private partnerships. Governments can also help to create an enabling environment for impact investing by promoting social entrepreneurship, innovation, and sustainable development.

- ***Mobilizing large pools of capital***
To achieve impact at scale, impact investors must mobilize large pools of capital. This can involve developing innovative financial instruments that enable investors to invest in impact-focused initiatives across different asset classes and geographies.

- ***Building infrastructure***

Impact investing requires the development of robust infrastructure to support investment activity. This includes the establishment of impact-focused investment funds, the creation of networks and platforms for impact investors to connect and collaborate, and the development of impact measurement and reporting frameworks.

- ***Catalyzing innovation***

To address complex global challenges, impact investors must catalyze innovation in a wide range of areas, including technology, social enterprise, and sustainable infrastructure. This can involve investing in early-stage companies and start-ups that are developing innovative solutions to pressing social and environmental issues.

- ***Fostering partnerships***

Scaling impact investing globally requires fostering partnerships between investors, governments, philanthropic organizations, and civil society. These partnerships can help to create an enabling environment for impact investing, unlock new sources of funding, and promote collaboration and knowledge-sharing.

- ***Addressing policy barriers***

Policymakers play a critical role in shaping the impact investing landscape. To scale impact investing globally, there is a need for policymakers to create regulatory frameworks that support impact investing activity, provide tax incentives to attract investment capital and promote the development of impact-focused investment vehicles.

- ***Promoting diversity, equity, and inclusion***

To achieve impact at scale, it is essential to promote diversity, equity, and inclusion in impact investing. This involves ensuring that investment activity is inclusive of all communities and that investments are made in a way that promotes social justice and equality.

- ***Empowering local communities***

Impact investing can have the greatest impact when it is driven by local communities. To scale impact investing globally, there is a need to empower local communities to take ownership of their development, invest in local solutions, and drive positive social and environmental change.

# CHAPTER SIX

**The Potential of Impact Investing to Drive Positive Change**

Impact investing has the potential to drive positive change by aligning financial interests with social and environmental outcomes. As such, impact investing represents a powerful tool for creating positive change and addressing some of the most pressing global challenges. Impact investing has the potential to drive positive change in several ways:

- *Mobilizing capital*

Impact investing can help to mobilize capital towards social and environmental causes, which can be critical in addressing pressing global challenges such as poverty, climate change, and inequality. By providing funding to organizations that are working to address these challenges, impact investing can help to accelerate progress toward a more sustainable and equitable future.

- ***Promoting innovation***

Impact investing can also promote innovation by providing funding to businesses and organizations that are developing new solutions to social and environmental challenges. By investing in these innovative ideas, impact investors can help to drive progress towards more sustainable and equitable systems.

- ***Encouraging responsible business practices***

Impact investing can also encourage responsible business practices by promoting environmental, social, and governance (ESG) criteria. By investing in companies that meet these criteria, impact investors can encourage more responsible business practices and help to mitigate risks.

- ***Creating positive financial returns***

Impact investing offers the potential for positive financial returns, which can help to attract more capital to support social and environmental causes. By demonstrating that impact investing can generate competitive financial returns, investors can help to shift more capital towards organizations that are making a positive difference.

- ***Driving systemic change***

Impact investing can also help to drive systemic change by promoting more sustainable and equitable business practices. By investing in businesses that prioritize social and environmental outcomes, impact investors can help to encourage other businesses to adopt similar practices.

- ***Supporting underserved communities***

Impact investing can help to support underserved communities by providing funding to organizations that are working to address social and economic inequality. By investing in these organizations, impact investors can help to provide resources and opportunities to communities that may otherwise be overlooked.

- *Aligning financial goals with social and environmental goals*

Impact investing can also help to align financial goals with social and environmental goals. By investing in organizations that are working to make a positive difference, impact investors can achieve both financial returns and positive social and environmental outcomes.

## The Need for Collaboration and Continued Innovation in Impact Investing

While impact investing has gained significant momentum in recent years, there is still a great need for collaboration and continued innovation to drive even greater impact. Collaboration is essential in impact investing because many of the most pressing social and environmental challenges we face are complex and interconnected. No single organization or investor can solve these challenges alone, which is why investors need to work together with other stakeholders such as governments, non-profits, and communities to drive meaningful change. Collaborative efforts can help to identify the most pressing issues, develop effective solutions, and scale impact more efficiently.

Furthermore, continued innovation is necessary to ensure that impact investing remains relevant and effective in addressing the ever-evolving social and environmental challenges of our time. Innovations can take many forms, such as new investment models, new technologies, and new approaches to impact measurement and reporting. For example, the rise of blockchain technology has opened up new opportunities for impact investing by enabling more secure and transparent transactions, while the development of new impact measurement frameworks can help investors better assess the social and environmental impact of their investments.

In addition to collaboration and innovation, impact investing also requires a long-term perspective. Many of the most pressing social and environmental challenges we face are deeply entrenched and complex, and solutions will require sustained effort over many years. Therefore, impact investors need to maintain a long-term focus and be patient in their pursuit of impact.

Overall, impact investing has the potential to drive significant positive change in the world, but it will require collaboration, innovation, and a long-term perspective to achieve its full potential. By working together and continuing to push the boundaries of what is possible, impact investors can help to create a more sustainable and equitable future for all.

Printed in Great Britain
by Amazon